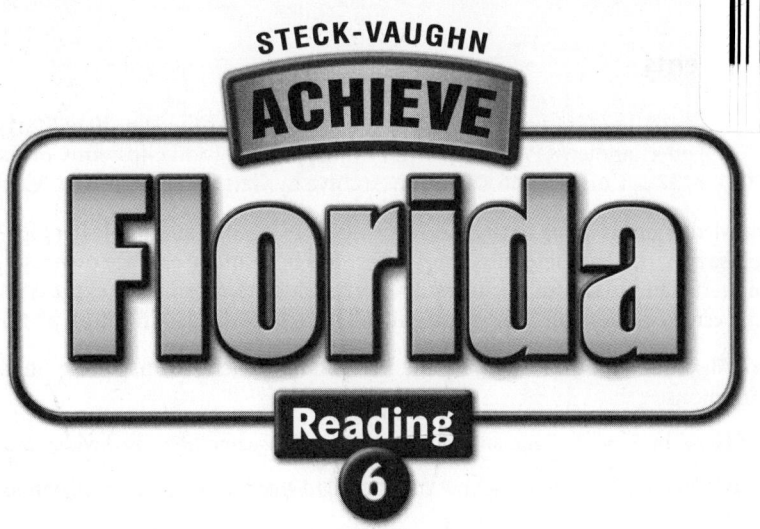

www.HarcourtAchieve.com
1.800.531.5015

Acknowledgments

Photography p. 4 © The Granger Collection; p. 6 © Brown Brothers; p. 30 © Marty Lederhandler/AP/Wide World Photos; p. 31 © Todd Gipstein/Corbis; p. 37 © Corbis; p. 46 © Hulton Archive by Getty Images; p. 47 © Corbis

Grateful acknowledgment is made to the following authors, agents, and publishers for permission to use copyrighted materials. Every effort has been made to trace ownership of all copyrighted material and to secure the necessary permissions to reprint. We express regret in advance for any error or omission. Any oversight will be acknowledged in future printings.

Authors: Carol Alexander, Judith Herbst, Estelle Kleinman, Marlene Roth, Sandra Shichtman, and Marren Simmons

"Jane's House of Hope" by Renée C. Rebman. Copyright PLAYS Magazine 1996, used with permission.

"Tackling the Trash" by Jill Esbaum. Copyright © 2002 by Highlights for Children, Inc., Columbus, Ohio.

"Growing Up on Ellis Island" by Margaret Macalister Slepkow. From APPLESEEDS' September 2001 issue: *Statue of Liberty,* © 2001, Cobblestone Publishing Company, 30 Grove Street, Suite C, Peterborough, NH 03458. All Rights Reserved. Reprinted by permission of Carus Publishing Group.

"Daybreak" from THREE BOOKS By Galway Kinnell. Copyright © 1993 by Galway Kinnell. Previously published in *Mortal Acts, Mortal Words* (1980). Reprinted by permission of Houghton Mifflin Company. All rights reserved.

"The Men Had All Gone to War" from RELUCTANT WITNESS by Emmy Werner. Copyright ©1998 by Westview Press. Reprinted by permission of Westview Press, a member of Perseus Books, L.L.C.

"Portrait by a Neighbour" by Edna St. Vincent Millay. Copyright © 1922, 1950 by Edna St. Vincent Millay.

From WHERE THE RED FERN GROWS: The Story of Two Dogs and a Boy by Wilson Rawls, copyright ©1961 by Sophie S. Rawls, Trustee, or successor Trustee(s) of the Rawls Trust, dated July 31, 1991. Copyright ©1961 by the Curtis Publishing Company. Used by permission of Random House Children's Books, a division of Random House.

"The Marble Champ" by Gary Soto. Excerpt from BASEBALL IN APRIL AND OTHER STORIES, copyright © 1990 by Gary Soto, reprinted by permission of Harcourt, Inc.

"Galileo and the Moons of Jupiter" by Tony Helies. Copyright ©2002 by Highlights for Children, Inc., Columbus, Ohio.

The FCAT is published by the Florida Department of Education. Such organization has neither endorsed nor authorized this test-preparation book.

ISBN 0-7398-8840-4

© 2005 Harcourt Achieve Inc.

All rights reserved. No part of the material protected by this copyright may be reproduced or utilized in any form or by any means, in whole or in part, without permission in writing from the copyright owner. Requests for permission should be mailed to: Copyright Permissions, Harcourt Achieve, P.O. Box 26015, Austin, TX 78755.

Rigby and Steck-Vaughn are trademarks of Harcourt Achieve Inc. registered in the United States of America and/or other jurisdictions.

1 2 3 4 5 6 7 8 9 10 073 11 10 09 08 07 06 05 04

Achieve Florida
Contents

Sunshine State Standards 2

To the Student 3

Modeled Instruction 4
    Session 1 4
    Session 2 13

Test-Taking Tips 22

FCAT Practice Test 23
    Session 1 25
    Session 2 41

Answer Sheet 59

Sunshine State Language Arts Standards

Achieve Florida will help you get ready for the Florida Comprehensive Assessment Test (FCAT), a test that has been based on the standards set up by the state of Florida. Standards are the goals that have been developed to make sure that you have all the skills necessary to be successful in school.

The Florida Comprehensive Assessment Test (FCAT) will ask you to respond to reading questions and writing prompts. Here is a brief description of the test and the standards that are measured.

Standard 1: You will show that you can use the reading process effectively.

- You will use clues to figure out the meaning of words.
- You will draw conclusions about passages.
- You will recognize the patterns of writing that authors use to organize and help you understand their work.

Standard 2: You will show that you can read and understand information from many different kinds of texts. You will read about different kinds of writing, including fiction, nonfiction, poetry, and drama.

- You will identify comparison and contrast within passages.
- You will determine the main idea and supporting details when you read.
- You will identify the author's purpose in writing.
- You will locate, choose, and gather information from a variety of reference materials for a number of different purposes.
- You will explain the difference between a fact and an opinion.
- You will show that you understand the relationship between cause and effect in fiction and nonfiction passages.
- You will show that you understand the elements of a story, including plot, character, point of view, and tone.
- You will show you understand how a story is developed through plot, complications, and resolution.

To The Student

This book will help you prepare for a test based on the Florida Comprehensive Assessment Test (FCAT). The first part of the book, Modeled Instruction, will give you practice on the different kinds of questions you will see on the real test. The Modeled Instruction will also give you tips for answering each question.

The second part of the book, the Practice Test, is similar to the actual FCAT. Taking the Practice Test will help you know what the actual FCAT is like.

The FCAT has questions about reading. It asks you to answer questions about what you have read. These test questions will help measure how well you understand the Sunshine State Standards.

Kinds of Items

Multiple-Choice Items

After each multiple-choice item are four answer choices. In Modeled Instruction, you will need to circle the letter of each correct answer. In the Practice Test, you will mark your answers on the Answer Sheet. Remember to pick the choice that you think is best.

Session 1 Modeled Instruction

Read the passage from the play *Jane's House of Hope* before answering Numbers 1 through 5.

from *Jane's House of Hope*

Renée C. Rebman

Jane Addams

Characters
    JANE ADDAMS, founder of Hull House
    ELLEN GATES STARR, her friend
    MR. STEVENS, estate agent

SCENE 1
    TIME: *Late 1800s*
    BEFORE RISE: *A small pool of light comes up on* JANE ADDAMS, *seated at a small desk right, in front of the curtain. She is writing a letter; she finishes, pauses, then reads aloud.*
JANE: Dear Ellen. My trip through Europe has been wonderful. I've seen the most beautiful palaces and cathedrals. I've also been saddened by the things I've seen in poverty-stricken neighborhoods.
    While walking through a slum of London, I witnessed the poor begging for tickets to a soup kitchen, and fighting over scraps of food unfit to eat. I cannot express how desperately I wish to help. I recently visited Toynbee Hall, a settlement house where the poor can take lessons, read books, and participate in cultural activities. I want to establish my own settlement house in Chicago. Would you be interested in helping me, dear Ellen? I am confident we can make a difference and provide a sanctuary for many. I am looking forward to my return to America and to your reply. Sincerely, Jane.
    (*She lowers letter and speaks.*) I do hope you'll help me, Ellen. (*Blackout*)
SCENE 2
    TIME: *1889*
    SETTING: *Large parlor at Hull House in Chicago, with sofa, a few chairs and small tables. Room is not meant to look lived in at this point. Exit right leads to other rooms. Working door left is front door to house.*
    AT RISE: JANE, ELLEN GATES STARR, *and* MR. STEVENS *enter.*
    MR. STEVENS: Well, ladies, I trust you've enjoyed your tour of Hull House. (*They all sit.*)

JANE: Yes, thank you, Mr. Stevens. The house is adequate for our needs.

ELLEN: It will do very nicely, indeed.

MR. STEVENS *(Hesitating)*: Ah, your needs...I'm not entirely clear on...

JANE: You seem uncomfortable, Mr. Stevens. Is there a problem?

MR. STEVENS: I must admit that when I received notice I had an appointment to show the house, I expected it was with a Mr. Addams. I'm not accustomed to showing real estate to women.

JANE: And I, sir, am not accustomed to this archaic way of thinking!

ELLEN *(Diplomatically)*: Forgive my friend, Mr. Stevens. She can be a bit overzealous at times. Is there anything we can say that would make you more comfortable about this?

MR. STEVENS: I feel I have a great responsibility to the owner of Hull House to assure him his property will be protected and respected. This idea of yours for a settlement house—inviting just anyone inside—it's...

JANE: By "just anyone," you're referring to the poor, aren't you, Mr. Stevens? I assure you, poverty does not automatically make a person a vandal or a criminal! It is only through education and opportunity that anyone can ever hope to rise above poverty. The people we want to help live right in this neighborhood. That's the main reason we're interested in this property. It's located where the help is needed the most.

ELLEN *(Sincerely)*: We realize the idea of a settlement house is new in this country, but while Jane was in England, she visited a successful settlement house, Toynbee Hall. *(Fervently)* It can work, Mr. Stevens. And it will.

MR. STEVENS: Your conviction is admirable, but it's such an enormous project.

ELLEN: We're up to the challenge. In fact, we welcome it.

JANE: We have a great deal of support in the community and we have the money, Mr. Stevens. All we need is a signed lease.

ELLEN *(Smiling)*: And only you can arrange the lease, Mr. Stevens. Please, will you help us?

MR. STEVENS *(Chuckling)*: Miss Starr, you're most ambitious; you also, Miss Addams—and most headstrong, I might add.

JANE: Thank you, sir. We'll take that as a compliment.

MR. STEVENS *(Smiling)*: It was intended as one...You'll have your lease by tomorrow morning.

ELLEN: Oh, thank you! *(Shakes Mr. Stevens' hand)*

JANE: Thank you, Mr. Stevens. *(Shakes his hand)* You won't be sorry.

MR. STEVENS: Make certain I'm not... *(Shakes head)* Young women these days; I suppose you'll be wanting the vote next!

ELLEN *(Bristling)*: And why not?

JANE: Forgive my friend, Mr. Stevens. She can be a bit overzealous.

MR. STEVENS: You two are a perfect match. *(Hands Jane a key)* Your key, Miss Addams. *(He exits.)*

ELLEN *(Hugging Jane)*: It's ours! It's really ours!

JANE: There's so much to do; this is only the beginning.

ELLEN: The beginning of many good things. *(They exit. Blackout)*

"Jane's House of Hope" by Renée C. Rebman. Copyright PLAYS Magazine 1996, used with permission.

Now answer Numbers 1 through 5. Circle the letter of the correct answer. Base your answers on the passage from Jane's House of Hope.

1 Read this sentence from the passage.

> **I am confident we can make a difference and provide a sanctuary for many.**

What is the meaning of *sanctuary* in this sentence?

- **A.** a holy or sacred place
- **B.** the inner rooms of a church
- **C.** a place of protection and aid for poor people
- **D.** a place where wild animals are safe and protected

Tip: Notice the kind of place that Toynbee Hall was. Think about the different activities offered there for the poor. Decide how Toynbee Hall is like a sanctuary.

2 Why does Jane Addams want to establish a settlement house in Chicago?

- **F.** to nurse people who are seriously ill
- **G.** to protect mothers and young children from violence
- **H.** to help poor people become educated and find jobs
- **I.** to help women gain the right to vote in national elections

Tip: Think about what kind of person Jane Addams was and what she believed in. Ask yourself what her goals were and how she wanted to achieve them.

Sunshine State Language Arts Standards
1. **LA.A.1.3.2:** Uses a variety of strategies to analyze words and text, draw conclusions, use context and word structure clues, and recognize organizational patterns.
2. **LA.A.2.3.1:** Determines the main idea or essential message in a text and identifies relevant details and facts and patterns of organization.

Go On

3 How are Jane Addams and Ellen Gates Starr alike?

  A. Both care much about the opinions of others.

  B. Both visited settlement houses in Europe.

  C. Both feel strongly about women's right to vote.

  D. Both want to promote a cause in which they believe.

> **Tip:** Two characters can be compared by making a short list of their qualities. Think about why Mr. Stevens calls the pair a "perfect match." Take a look at the two women's words and actions just before he makes this comment.

4 Why does Mr. Stevens give the women the lease?

  F. He thinks that their plan will fail.

  G. He likes what they intend to do with the place.

  H. He is impressed by their vision and determination.

  I. He believes that women are more responsible than men.

> **Tip:** Usually important plot details can be found by rereading a passage. Go back and look at Scene 2 again. Think about what the women say and do to convince Mr. Stevens to give them the lease.

5 Why does the author retell the episode between Mr. Stevens, Jane Addams, and Ellen Gates Starr?

  A. to show that Jane had difficulty getting along with others

  B. to show that the women were determined to help the poor and change society's attitude toward them

  C. to show that women could be as successful in business as men

  D. to show that it was difficult to find a suitable building in which to establish a settlement house

> **Tip:** Authors show their purpose through their characters. Also, think about the ideas the author seems to value. Consider how the author probably feels about Addams and Gates Starr and the way Mr. Stevens treats them.

Sunshine State Language Arts Standards
3. **LA.A.2.2.7** Recognizes the use of comparison and contrast in a text.
4. **LA.E.2.3.1** Understands how character and plot development, point of view, and tone are used in various selections to support a central conflict or story line.
5. **LA.A.2.3.2** Identifies the author's purpose and/or point of view in a variety of texts and uses the information to construct meaning.

Go On

The Men Had All Gone to War

Emmy E. Werner

During the American Civil War (1861–1865), the Union Army set up a blockade so that the South could not receive shipments of arms, food, clothing, and other basic necessities. This was done in order to make the war end more quickly. Sadly, many innocent people had to go hungry and cold during those difficult years.

New Year's Day 1863 promised freedom to the slaves, but no end to the war between the North and South. In the Confederacy[1], food and other necessities of life had become scarce; the blockade of Southern ports by the Union navy was beginning to take its toll on civilians and soldiers alike.

Ten-year-old Evelyn Ward of Bladensfield, Virginia, remembered: "About this time supplies began to be very scarce. There was no sugar or coffee or tea, no new calicos or cotton. There were no men to keep the stores…they had all gone to the War." But her parents found ways of making the limited supplies last as long as possible. Wrote this little girl:

> Mother…had rye toasted with just enough coffee to flavor it to make the coffee hold out. Father planted a big patch of sorghum.[2]…Mr. Mothershead …got a mill to grind it and boil the juice down to make molasses.…It made fine molasses, and Sylvia made good gingerbread with it.… When all the candies were gone from the stores, we made taffy of sorghum, and after the…nights had become frosty, we used to cut down a sorghum cane, peel off a joint, and chew the pith.

The food shortage was beginning to reach from the countryside into the Southern towns and cities. In Richmond a government clerk noted in his journal:

> Some idea may be formed of the scarcity of food in this city from the fact that while my youngest daughter was in the kitchen today, a young rat came out of its hole and seemed to beg for something to eat; she held out some bread which it ate from her hand and seemed grateful. Several others soon appeared and were as tame as kittens.

…As the Northern blockade held, prices in the Confederacy continued to rise at the rate of ten percent a month. Scarcity made Southern women inventive. They made needles from hawthorn bushes, paint brushes from hog bristles, rope from Spanish moss, red dye from figs, and tea from raspberry leaves. They substituted coffee with ground acorns, beets, chicory, corn, okra, peas, and pumpkin seeds—"all that is wanted is something to color the water."

Said a young Richmond girl: "We are starving. As soon as enough of us get together we are going to take the bakeries and each of us will take a loaf of bread. That is little enough for the government to give us after it has taken all our men."

On April 2, 1863, nearly a thousand women and children in Richmond banded together and "marched along silently and in order." They methodically[3] emptied stores of goods and ignored the pleading of the mayor and the presence of Confederate troops. In desperation, Confederate President Jefferson Davis appeared and spoke "with great kindness and sympathy." The women moved on, taking their food with them. Over forty-eight hours later, an observer noted, "Women and children are still standing in the streets, demanding food." Similar incidents took place in the capital cities of Alabama and Georgia and in North and South Carolina.

---

[1]**Confederacy:** the eleven Southern states that left the United States in 1860 and 1861
[2]**sorghum:** a grass with solid stems and many grains
[3]**methodically:** in an orderly fashion

"The Men Had All Gone to War" from RELUCTANT WITNESS by Emmy Werner. Copyright ©1998 by Westview Press. Reprinted by permission of Westview Press, a member of Perseus Books, L.L.C.

Now answer Numbers 6 through 10. Circle the letter of the correct answer. Base your answers on the passage "The Men Had All Gone to War."

6 Why does the author give details about the kinds of foods many Southerners ate during the war?

F. to show how new recipes are invented
G. to show why the South could not win the Civil War
H. to show how people cope in times of a food shortage
I. to show that Northerners and Southerners prepared different foods

Tip: Many times an author's purpose can be found by looking at the details. Examine the details in the passage and draw your own conclusions. Think about why the details about foods available to Southerners would be important to the author.

7 According to the passage, which of these is an effect of the blockade?

A. a return to simple foods
B. increasing prices in the South
C. new respect for the Confederacy
D. an increase in the rat population

Tip: Often the main idea of a passage is related to the effects of an action. As you review the passage, jot down a list of effects created by the blockade. Notice what all the effects have in common.

Sunshine State Language Arts Standards
6. **LA.A.2.3.2:** Identifies the author's purpose and/or point of view in a variety of texts and uses the information to construct meaning.
7. **LA.A.2.3.1:** Determines the main idea or essential message in a text and identifies relevant details and facts and patterns of organization.

8 Which of the following best describes this passage?

- F. It is based mostly on facts.
- G. It is based mostly on opinions.
- H. It is based on weak supporting details.
- I. It is based on the personal values of the author.

Tip: You can make a general statement about a passage by reviewing its content. Look at the topic sentences and details. Ask yourself what type of information is being presented. In your review, look for facts, opinions, details, and the author's conclusions.

9 What was the author's purpose in writing this passage?

- A. to describe how Southern women helped the war effort
- B. to persuade readers that the North used unfair tactics against the South
- C. to explain the effects of the Northern blockade on the South
- D. to entertain readers with stories of the American Civil War

Tip: Remember, an author does not always state his or her purpose. If an author has succeeded at persuading or entertaining you, or explaining or describing something, then you can figure out the purpose of the passage.

10 This passage could best be used for a student research project on

- F. world food shortages.
- G. effective Civil War tactics.
- H. the battles of the Civil War.
- I. Confederate President Jefferson Davis.

Tip: Readers use passages for reports based on the main topic of each passage. Scan the passage to determine the general message. Ask yourself what report topic this passage would best support.

Sunshine State Language Arts Standards
8. **LA.A.2.3.8:** Checks the validity and accuracy of information obtained from research, in such ways as differentiating fact and opinion, identifying strong vs. weak arguments, and recognizing that personal values influence the conclusions an author draws.
9. **LA.A.2.3.2:** Identifies the author's purpose and/or point of view in a variety of texts and uses the information to construct meaning.
10. **LA.A.2.3.5:** Locates, organizes, and interprets written information for a variety of purposes, including classroom research, collaborative decision-making, and performing a school or real-world task.

12 • Modeled Instruction

Session 2 Modeled Instruction

Read the poem "The Echoing Green" before answering Numbers 11 through 16.

The Echoing Green

William Blake

The sun does arise,
And make happy the skies;
The merry bells ring
To welcome the Spring;
The skylark and thrush,
The birds of the bush,
Sing louder around,
To the bells' cheerful sound,
While our sports shall be seen,
On the Echoing Green[1].
Old John, with white hair,
Does laugh away care,
Sitting under the oak,
Among the old folk.
They laugh at our play,
And soon they all say:

[1] **green:** grassy land

"Such, such were the joys
When we all, girls and boys,
In our youth-time were seen,
On the Echoing Green."
Till the little ones, weary,
No more can be merry;
The sun does descend,
And our sports have an end.
Round the laps of their mothers,
Many sisters and brothers,
Like birds in their nest,
Are ready for rest,
And sport no more seen,
On the darkening Green.

Now answer Numbers 11 through 16. Circle the letter of the correct answer. Base your answers on the poem "The Echoing Green."

11 This poem is told from the point of view of

   A. a child.
   B. Old John.
   C. one of the parents.
   D. an unknown speaker.

> **Tip:** In poetry, the point of view is the view of the person speaking. It is not always clear who the speaker is. Look for clues, like pronouns (I, my, our, we). Figure out the age of the speaker and what is important to him or her.

12 What causes the children to stop playing?

   F. They are bored.
   G. They are tired.
   H. The old people laugh at them.
   I. Their mothers call them home.

> **Tip:** Causes and effects are usually listed in order, even when the author does not use clue words. To find why the children stop playing, reread the poem and note each event. Think about what causes the children to stop playing.

13 What is the tone of this poem?

   A. bitter
   B. formal
   C. apologetic
   D. lighthearted

> **Tip:** Tone is a general attitude or feeling that the author shows in a passage. Writers often use certain words or phrases to help them show the tone. To find the tone, look at the words and images that the speaker uses.

Sunshine State Language Arts Standards
11. **LA.E.2.3.1:** Understands how character and plot development, point of view, and tone are used in various selections to support a central conflict or story line.
12. **LA.E.2.2.1:** Recognizes cause-and-effect relationships in literary texts.
13. **LA.E.2.3.1:** Understands how character and plot development, point of view, and tone are used in various selections to support a central conflict or story line.

14 Which of the following is the best summary of the poem?

- F. The birds of spring sing along with the sound of cheerful bells.
- G. Old folks sit under an oak tree and think about their childhoods.
- H. Children play on the green from sunrise to sunset as old folks watch.
- I. Sleepy young children go back to their mothers as the sun goes down.

Tip: Sometimes poets ask you to draw conclusions from the details they include. You can use the details of the poem to understand the main idea. Review the poem and identify the events that happen. Then ask yourself what the poem is about.

15 The poet wishes to express which human experience in the poem?

- A. the hardships of old age
- B. the carefree joy of childhood
- C. regret for lost opportunities
- D. the uncertainty of people's lives

Tip: Poets use words and images in a special way to show their purpose rather than stating it directly. Think about what is probably most important to the poet. Review the details and images in the poem to discover the author's purpose.

16 To what are the children compared at the end of the poem?

- F. the old folk
- G. birds in their nest
- H. merry ringing bells
- I. the darkening Green

Tip: Remember the words *as* or *like* are often used to compare two or more things. Scan the text for the words *as* or *like* to find the comparison.

Sunshine State Language Arts Standards
14. LA.A.2.3.1: Determines the main idea or essential message in a text and identifies relevant details and facts and patterns of organization.
15. LA.A.2.3.2: Identifies the author's purpose and/or point of view in a variety of texts and uses the information to construct meaning.
16. LA.A.2.2.7: Recognizes the use of comparison and contrast in a text.

Go On

16 • Modeled Instruction

Read the article "Tackling the Trash" before answering Numbers 17 through 21.

Tackling the Trash

Jill Esbaum

Not many people would spend their free time picking up other people's litter. But Chad Pregracke has spent most of the past five years doing just that along the Mississippi, Ohio, and Illinois rivers.

Why?

Chad grew up in a house alongside the Mississippi. He loved to fish and camp on the river's wooded islands. That's when he first noticed the junk dotting its shoreline. Many other boaters and campers used the river, too. Unfortunately, some of them didn't care where they threw their trash.

Spring floods added to the clutter. When flood waters went down, they left behind everything from tin cans to 55-gallon steel drums, from tires to TV sets.

"It was getting worse every year," Chad says. "And nobody was cleaning it up."

In May of 1997, Chad came home from college for summer vacation. As usual, he was disgusted by the junk that littered the riverbanks near his hometown of East Moline, Illinois. But this time, instead of wondering why someone else didn't clean it up, he decided to tackle a few miles of shoreline himself.

With only a flat-bottom boat, a wheelbarrow, and a sturdy pair of gloves, he motored up and down the river. Whenever he spotted trash, he pulled to shore and picked it up. When his boat was full, he took the load to a landfill. Chad even took pictures of the junk he hauled away. "I thought it might be fun to see how much trash I could pick up," he says.

Soon the riverbanks near his hometown were litter-free. And Chad was hooked. "I really enjoyed it," he says. "I could see the results day after day. It made me feel good to help my community." So he kept going, sleeping under a tarp each night.

But Chad's money was disappearing fast. Food, gasoline for his boat, landfill charges, and film costs were gobbling up his resources. He wondered if others would help support his cleanup.

First Chad talked to government agencies like the National Fish and Wildlife Service and the U.S. Army Corps of Engineers. While happy about his work, they didn't have much money to donate.

So Chad called area businesses. He explained about growing up beside the river, the mess it had become, and his determination to clean it up. Most companies wouldn't help either. But finally one company decided to lend a hand. Chad got his first small grant and the encouragement he needed to find others to help as well.

Chad began visiting other companies in person and found that his careful record keeping paid off. People couldn't help being impressed by his enthusiasm, or by the pictures of the junk he'd already hauled away. The next year, Chad received enough money to finish his summer's work with several volunteers to help him. In two years he raised enough money to buy two more boats and hire five helpers for the next summer.

In 1998, Chad's goal was to clean 1,000 miles of shoreline. Beginning in northern Iowa, he and his crew slowly worked their way south. Their final destination was St. Louis, Missouri. Along the way, Chad had to receive permission from each town to pile his junk in a parking lot or field. When he finished each area, he trucked the trash to the nearest landfill.

As the hot summer wore on, the work became more difficult. The farther south they traveled, the more trash littered the shore. One mile of shoreline was so full of old tires, it took more than a month to clean—one small boatload at a time. Sheltered only by tents and tarps, Chad and his crew battled mosquitoes and summer storms. By summer's end only Chad and one helper remained on the job. When cold weather forced them to stop, they were just fifty miles from St. Louis.

Chad didn't spend the winter months catching up on sleep. He needed to raise more than $100,000. Part of the money would go toward finishing his work near St. Louis. The rest would fund his next project, cleaning the 270-mile shoreline of the Illinois River.

Go On

Chad also traveled from town to town. He spoke at schools, churches, and town halls. He shared his story with community groups, conservation clubs, and Scout troops. He asked them to help keep the river clean.

People were eager to help. Someone even offered him a used houseboat for free. There was only one catch: it was resting on the muddy bottom of the Illinois River. "It was a real mess," Chad remembers. "The most totally trashed thing you've seen in your life."

After a lot of repair work and elbow grease, *The Miracle* became the crew's floating home and headquarters—a big step up from tents and tarps.

In 2000, Chad began hosting community-wide cleanup days in cities along the Mississippi. "I want to get as many people involved as possible," he says.

Toward that goal, Chad encourages individuals and community groups to participate in his Adopt-a-Mississippi-Mile program, pledging to keep a mile of shoreline litter-free.

Chad did return to college in 2001 and received his associate's degree. But for now, Chad is devoting himself to the river and cleaning it up has taken over his life.

But he doesn't mind one bit. "I work with good people who have become my best friends," he says. "I love it."

This is a partial list of items Chad has pulled out of the rivers:

18 duck decoys
348 bottles of antifreeze
8 anchors
13 air conditioners
28 toilets
350 propane tanks
56 stoves
46 washing machines
223 milk crates
14,240 pounds of metal
28 garbage cans
4,870 car tires
55 life jackets
13 baby pools

968 buckets
287 refrigerators
1,109 55-gallon steel drums
27 bicycles
40 barbecue grills
430 feet of steel cable
15 boat bumpers
75 water heaters
307 chairs
171 coolers
2 swing sets
49 sinks
72 TV sets

"Tackling the Trash" by Jill Esbaum. Copyright © 2002 by Highlights for Children, Inc., Columbus, Ohio.

Now answer Numbers 17 through 21. Circle the letter of the correct answer. Base your answers on the article "Tackling the Trash."

17 What first caused Chad to seek support from others for his cleanup?

A. He was running out of money.

B. He thought he could do a better job with some help.

C. He wanted to spend less personal time on the cleanup.

D. He wanted to start a national movement to clean up the rivers.

> **Tip:** Sometimes important details in a passage show causes or effects. Go back and review Chad's actions. Think about what happened right before Chad talked to some agencies and companies.

18 The events in this article are presented in

F. chronological order.

G. order of importance.

H. cause-and-effect order.

I. problem-solution order.

> **Tip:** Writers of nonfiction use different patterns to present information in a way that makes sense. Chronological order tells events in the order they happened. Order of importance presents the most important idea first. Cause-and-effect order identifies causes and their effects. Problem-solution order presents a problem and then suggests a solution.

Sunshine State Language Arts Standards
17. **LA.A.2.3.1:** Determines the main idea or essential message in a text and identifies relevant details and facts and patterns of organization.
18. **LA.A.2.3.1:** Determines the main idea or essential message in a text and identifies relevant details and facts and patterns of organization.

19 What was the author's purpose in writing this article?

   A. to describe the type of litter found in the rivers
   B. to explain the reasons why people litter the rivers
   C. to discuss the problem of litter in American rivers
   D. to describe how one person helped clean up the rivers

> **Tip:** Remember, a writer's purpose may be to entertain, to express ideas, to persuade, or to inform. Think about why a writer would talk about Chad and his river clean-up project.

20 Which statement provides the best evidence of Chad's commitment to cleaning up the river?

   F. He took pictures of the junk he hauled away.
   G. He visited area businesses to get money for the cleanup.
   H. He finished college but still spends his time cleaning up the river.
   I. He hosted community-wide cleanup days in cities along the Mississippi.

> **Tip:** Some supporting details are stronger than others. Think about what it means to be committed to an idea. Ask yourself what detail is the strongest support for the idea. Decide which is the best evidence of Chad's commitment.

21 The information in this article could best be used for a research project about

   A. causes of water pollution
   B. how to find a summer job
   C. types of government programs
   D. how individuals affect the environment

> **Tip:** When you prepare a research report, you may read a variety of sources. Think about a report topic that would be supported by information from this passage.

Sunshine State Language Arts Standards
19. **LA.A.2.3.2:** Identifies the author's purpose and/or point of view in a variety of texts and uses the information to construct meaning.
20. **LA.A.2.3.8:** Checks the validity and accuracy of information obtained from research in such ways as differentiating fact and opinion, identifying strong vs. weak arguments, and recognizing that personal values influence the conclusions an author draws.
21. **LA.A.2.3.5:** Locates, organizes, and interprets written information for a variety of purposes, including classroom research, collaborative decision-making, and performing a school or real-world task.

Test-Taking Tips

Now you are ready to take a Practice Test for the Florida Comprehensive Assessment Test (FCAT). This practice test is similar to the reading portion of the FCAT. This practice test should help you feel more relaxed when you take the actual FCAT. Use what you learned in the first section of this book to help you succeed on this test.

Try using the following tips as you take the Practice Test:

- Read the directions and ask questions if you do not understand something.

- Read the passages and all the answer choices carefully. You may look back at the passage to help you answer the questions.

- With each passage, answer the questions you are sure about first. Then, you can go back to answer any question that seems too difficult at first.

- Record your answers on the Answer Sheet. Be sure to fill in the answer bubbles completely. If you want to change your answer, be sure to erase your first answer completely.

- Check to see that your answers are the best answers for the questions asked.

- Use any time remaining to review your answers.

- Relax and do your best. Practicing for the FCAT will help you.

FCAT Language Arts Practice Test

Table of Contents

from *Where the Red Fern Grows* 25

Growing Up on Ellis Island 30

Daybreak 34

Lighter Than Air 37

The Marble Champ 41

Galileo and the Moons of Jupiter 46

Portrait by a Neighbour 50

from *The Story of My Life* 53

After you have read each story, passage, or poem, read the questions and then answer them on the Answer Sheet.

Session 1

Read the passage from *Where the Red Fern Grows* before answering Numbers 1 through 8.

from *Where the Red Fern Grows*
The Story of Two Dogs and a Boy

Wilson Rawls

The dog-wanting disease never did leave me altogether. With the new work I was doing, helping Papa, it just kind of burned itself down and left a big sore on my heart. Every time I'd see a coon track down in our fields, or along the riverbanks, the old sore would get all festered up and start hurting again.

Just when I had given up all hope of ever owning a good hound, something wonderful happened. The good Lord figured I had hurt enough, and it was time to lend a helping hand.

It all started one day while I was hoeing corn down in our field close to the river. Across the river, a party of fishermen had been camped for several days. I heard the old Maxwell car as it snorted and chugged its way out of the bottoms. I knew they were leaving. Throwing down my hoe, I ran down to the river and waded across at a place called the Shannon Ford. I hurried to the camp ground.

It was always a pleasure to prowl where fishermen had camped. I usually could find things: a fish line, or a forgotten fish pole. On one occasion, I found a beautiful knife stuck in the bark of a sycamore tree, forgotten by a careless fisherman. But on that day, I found the greatest of treasures, a sportsman's magazine, discarded by the campers. It was a real treasure for a country boy. Because of that magazine, my entire life was changed.

I sat down on an old sycamore log and started thumbing through the leaves. On the back pages of the magazine, I came to the "For Sale" section— "Dogs for Sale"—every kind of dog. I read on and on. They had dogs I had never heard of, names I couldn't make out. Far down in the right-hand corner, I found an ad that took my breath away. In small letters, it read: "Registered redbone coon hound pups—twenty-five dollars each."

The advertisement was from a kennel in Kentucky. I read it over and over. By the time I had memorized the ad, I was seeing dogs, hearing dogs, and even feeling them. The magazine was forgotten. I was lost in thought. The brain of an eleven-year-old boy can dream some fantastic dreams.

How wonderful it would be if I could have two of those pups. Every boy in the country but me had a good hound or two. But fifty dollars—how could I ever get fifty dollars? I knew I couldn't expect help from Mama and Papa.

When I left the camp ground of the fishermen, it was late. As I walked along, I could feel the hard bulge of the magazine jammed deep in the pocket of my overalls. The beautiful silence that follows the setting sun had settled over the river bottoms. The coolness of the rich, black soil felt good to my bare feet.

It was the time of day when all furried things come to life. A big swamp rabbit hopped out on the trail, sat on his haunches, stared at me, and then scampered away. A mother gray squirrel ran out on the limb of a burr oak tree. She barked a warning to the four furry balls behind her. They melted from sight in the thick green. A silent gray shadow drifted down from the top of a tall sycamore. There was a squeal and a beating of wings. I heard

the tinkle of a bell in the distance ahead. I knew it was Daisy, our milk cow. I'd have to start her on the way home.

I took the magazine from my pocket and again I read the ad. Slowly a plan began to form. I'd save the money. I could sell stuff to the fishermen: crawfish, minnows, and fresh vegetables. In berry season, I could sell all the berries I could pick at my grandfather's store. I could trap in the winter. The more I planned, the more real it became. There was the way to get those pups—save my money.

I could almost feel the pups in my hands. I planned the little doghouse, and where to put it. Collars I could make myself. Then the thought came, "What could I name them?" I tried name after name, voicing them out loud. None seemed to fit. Well, there would be plenty of time for names.

Right now there was something more important—fifty dollars—a fabulous sum—a fortune—far more money than I had ever seen. Somehow, some way, I was determined to have it. I had twenty-three cents—a dime I had earned running errands for my grandpa, and thirteen cents a fisherman had given me for a can of worms.

The next morning I went to the trash pile behind the barn. I was looking for a can—my bank. I picked up several, but they didn't seem to be what I wanted. Then I saw it, an old K. C. Baking Powder can.

I dropped the twenty-three cents in the can. The coins looked so small lying there on the shiny bottom, but to me it was a good start. With my finger, I tried to measure how full it would be with fifty dollars in it.

…All through that summer I worked like a beaver. In the small creek that wormed its way down through our fields, I caught crawfish with my bare hands. I trapped minnows with an old screen-wire trap I made myself, baited with yellow corn bread from my mother's kitchen. These were sold to the fishermen, along with fresh vegetables and roasting ears. I tore my way through the blackberry patches until my hands and feet were scratched raw and red from the thorns. I tramped the hills seeking out the huckleberry bushes. My grandfather paid me ten cents a bucket for my berries.

…That winter I trapped harder than ever with the three little traps I owned. Grandpa sold my hides to fur buyers who came to his store all through the fur season. Prices were cheap: fifteen cents for a large opossum hide, twenty-five for a good skunk hide.

Little by little, the nickels and dimes added up. The old K. C. Baking Powder can grew heavy. I would heft its weight in the palm of my hand. With a straw, I'd measure from the lip of the can to the money. As the months went by, the straws grew shorter and shorter.

…A year passed. I was twelve. I was over the halfway mark. I had twenty-seven dollars and forty-six cents. My spirits soared. I worked harder.

Another year crawled slowly by, and then the great day came. The long hard grind was over. I had it—my fifty dollars! I cried as I counted it over and over.

From WHERE THE RED FERN GROWS: *The Story of Two Dogs and a Boy* by Wilson Rawls, copyright ©1961 by Sophie S. Rawls, Trustee, or successor Trustee(s) of the Rawls Trust, dated July 31, 1991. Copyright ©1961 by the Curtis Publishing Company. Used by permission of Random House Children's Books, a division of Random House.

Now answer Numbers 1 through 8. Mark your answers on the Answer Sheet. Base your answers on the passage from *Where the Red Fern Grows*.

1 Read this sentence from the passage.

But on that day, I found the greatest of treasures, a sportsman's magazine, discarded by the campers.

What does the word *discarded* mean?

A. lost

B. torn up

C. purchased

D. thrown away

2 Which words best describe the narrator?

F. hesitant and shy

G. sly and secretive

H. determined and resourceful

I. generous and compassionate

3 What causes the narrator to put a plan into effect to buy two dogs?

A. his deep desire for a pet

B. his new job working with his father

C. reading an ad in a sportsman's magazine

D. finding a K.C. Baking Powder can in the trash pile

4 With which statement would the author of this passage most likely agree?

F. The narrator deserves to get the dogs that he wants.

G. The narrator does not understand the responsibilities of owning two dogs.

H. The narrator should find a better way to spend his time than on trying to buy two dogs.

I. The narrator should be grateful to his parents for making him work for what he wants.

Go On ▶

28 ● Practice Test

5 Read this sentence from the passage.

All through that summer I worked like a beaver.

The narrator compares himself to a beaver to indicate that he

A. needed help.

B. worked hard.

C. knew what he was doing.

D. had confidence in himself.

6 Which of the following can you conclude about the narrator's family?

F. They do not want the narrator to have the dogs.

G. They do not have very much money.

H. They want the narrator to be happy.

I. They are very strict with the narrator.

7 What is the best evidence that the dogs mean a great deal to the narrator?

A. He thinks about different names for his dogs.

B. He reads about dogs for sale in a magazine.

C. He asks his grandfather to sell hides for him.

D. He works hard to earn the money to buy the dogs.

8 If you wanted to find out more information about redbone coon hounds, which of the following books would be most useful?

F. *Show Dogs*

G. *Hunting Dogs*

H. *Raccoons in the Wild*

I. *Dog Care and Grooming*

Go On

Read the article "Growing Up on Ellis Island" before answering Numbers 9 through 14.

Growing Up on Ellis Island

Margaret Macalister Slepkow

After sailing past the Statue of Liberty, immigrants stopped at Ellis Island to be "processed." Here they waited in long lines to answer questions and have medical inspections. After processing, immigrants either were given permission to stay in the United States or were returned to their homeland. At times, immigrants might stay on Ellis Island for days or weeks while they awaited a decision. However, most visits lasted only a few hours.

Today the island is home to the Ellis Island Immigration Museum. The museum's Oral History Project has recorded hundreds of interviews with immigrants, employees, and kids who lived there. These voices give us a glimpse of life on Ellis Island.

For the few American kids who lived there, Ellis Island was a unique home. These children of employees befriended new immigrants, traveled often on the Ellis Island Ferry, and boasted the Statue of Liberty as a next-door neighbor.

In the 1930s, Seymour's father was an Ellis Island doctor. The captain of the ferry, which connected the island to Manhattan, sometimes let Seymour pilot the boat. "I had the wheel to myself. The captain would stand by and point the boat and say, 'just go that way.' I'd blow the whistle."

Ellis Island

Go On

In the 1950s, Bill often rode the ferry to school in Manhattan. "I would help them tie up the boats. I would watch every move they made as they docked. The captain would let me put my hands on the steering wheel."

A different world existed in Ellis Island's underground passageways. These tunnels were used to transport supplies and people during bad weather. They also made ideal playgrounds. And with few kids on the island, adults sometimes substituted as playmates.

An Italian immigrant showed Seymour one of his favorite pastimes. "If I took laundry carts, I could make the equivalent of a skateboard by going down and quickly turning the corners of the passageways. I had a great time. Of course, this caused problems when they wanted to have the carts back."

Seymour also spent time with Mary, an Irish woman who mended hospital gowns. "She had her sewing machine in a dark cavern of a room, stacked with hundreds and hundreds of garments. One of my favorite things was to hide in the stacks of hospital garments. There were mountains of them down there, and, of course, they were coming from all sorts of sick wards, but they were very inviting."

Christmas on the island was special. Ruth's family attended services in the main building's Registry Room. A gigantic Christmas tree was placed at the end of the hall. Immigrants, employees, and their families sang carols. Scripture, printed in different languages, was passed out to the immigrants.

Perhaps most special of all was the comfort offered by the neighboring Statue of Liberty. "She was my big sister in bronze," Seymour remembers. "I would go out and watch her light up at night, and it was a great thrill. She was out there protecting me."

Though his view was of her back, this only added to his memory. "I had a special view of how she came on at dusk, and I knew that while everyone else owned her, and while the light would come on across the harbor and across the world, only I was seeing her from my vantage point. And that was very special."

Ellis Island ferry and the Statue of Liberty

"Growing Up on Ellis Island" by Margaret Macalister Slepkow. From APPLESEEDS' September 2001 issue: *Statue of Liberty,* © 2001, Cobblestone Publishing Company, 30 Grove Street, Suite C, Peterborough, NH 03458. All Rights Reserved. Reprinted by permission of Carus Publishing Group.

Now answer Numbers 9 through 14. Mark your answer on the Answer Sheet. Base your answers on the article "Growing Up on Ellis Island."

9 Which statement from the article best conveys its main idea?

A. Christmas on the island was special.

B. Today the island is home to the Ellis Island Immigration Museum.

C. For the few American kids who lived there, Ellis Island was a unique home.

D. After sailing past the Statue of Liberty, immigrants stopped at Ellis Island to be "processed."

10 According to the article, why did some children live at Ellis Island?

F. They were the children of Ellis Island employees.

G. They worked on the island mending hospital gowns and piloting ships.

H. They failed the medical inspections and were sent to the Ellis Island hospital.

I. They lived on Ellis Island before it became a place where immigrants were "processed."

11 What was the author's purpose in writing this article?

A. to describe the efforts taken by American children to make immigrants feel at home on Ellis Island

B. to inform readers what life was like for American children living on Ellis Island

C. to compare life for children on Ellis Island with that of children living in New York City

D. to convince children to visit the Ellis Island Immigration Museum

12 Read this sentence from the article.

"If I took laundry carts, I could make the equivalent of a skateboard by going down and quickly turning the corners of the passageways."

What would be the *equivalent* of a nickel?

F. a dime

G. a penny

H. five pennies

I. four quarters

13 Which of these statements from the article is an OPINION?

A. Scripture, printed in different languages, was passed out to the immigrants.

B. And with few kids on the island, adults sometimes substituted as playmates.

C. At times, immigrants might stay on Ellis Island for days or weeks while they awaited a decision.

D. Perhaps most special of all was the comfort offered by the neighboring Statue of Liberty.

14 If you wanted to find out more information about the underground passageways on Ellis Island, which of the following index entries would be the most useful?

F. Ellis Island, medical care, 112–118

G. Ellis Island, transporting supplies, 95–98

H. Ellis Island, immigrant processing, 24–36

I. Ellis Island, Oral History Project, 138–145

Read the poem "Daybreak" before answering Numbers 15 through 20.

Daybreak

Galway Kinnell

On the tidal mud, just before sunset,
dozens of starfishes
were creeping. It was
as though the mud were a sky
and enormous, imperfect stars
moved across it as slowly
as the actual stars cross heaven.
All at once they stopped,
and as if they had simply
increased their receptivity[1]
to gravity they sank down
into the mud; they faded down
into it and lay still; and by the time
pink of sunset broke across them
they were invisible
as the true stars at daybreak.

[1]receptivity: ability to receive

"Daybreak" from THREE BOOKS By Galway Kinnell. Copyright © 1993 by Galway Kinnell. Previously published in *Mortal Acts, Mortal Words* (1980). Reprinted by permission of Houghton Mifflin Company. All rights reserved.

Go On

Now answer Numbers 15 through 20. Mark your answer on the Answer Sheet. Base your answers on the poem "Daybreak."

15 Which are being compared in this poem?

  A. the sea and the sky

  B. mud and clouds

  C. starfish and stars

  D. sunset and daybreak

16 How do the starfish come onto the beach?

  F. They swim out of the ocean.

  G. They wash ashore during storms.

  H. They dig up from beneath the sand.

  I. They are brought in with the evening tide.

17 Read these lines from the poem.

**All at once they stopped,
and as if they had simply
increased their receptivity
to gravity they sank down
into the mud. . . .**

The poet suggests the starfish sank down as if they

  A. were being stepped on.

  B. had gotten much larger.

  C. were being pulled downward.

  D. became frozen and couldn't move.

Go On

Practice Test • 35

18 What was the poet's purpose in writing this poem?

- F. to inform readers about starfish
- G. to express a deeply felt emotion about starfish
- H. to persuade readers to learn more about sea life
- I. to paint a mental picture of the starfish on the beach

19 What is the tone of this poem?

- A. somber and bitter
- B. amused and doubtful
- C. mean and critical
- D. relaxed and peaceful

20 Read this line from the poem.

**On the tidal mud, just before sunset,
dozens of starfishes
were creeping.**

What does the word *tidal* mean?

- F. neat and clean
- G. affected by ocean
- H. near the beach
- I. washed and dried

Read the article "Lighter Than Air" before answering Numbers 21 through 28.

Lighter Than Air

UFO buffs love to talk about the "strange airships" that appeared in the skies between 1896 and 1897. These vessels must have contained visitors from another planet, they claim, since we did not develop airships until World War I. This is simply nonsense. Although it is true that the first notable airships appeared after 1914, there were airships in the skies before that time. The first airship most people remember is the *Graf Zeppelin*, which flew on a regular basis between 1928 and 1937. However, it was back in 1852 that Henri Giffard flew a steam-powered airship between Paris and Trappes. Another Frenchman, Pierre Jullien, built and successfully tested two clockwork-driven, gas-filled airships in the 1850s. So it's a safe bet that the airships sighted around the turn of the century did not contain aliens.

The first airship

Lighter-than-air aircraft drift in the air due to the buoyancy of a balloon. The balloon is filled with a gas lighter than the air it displaces. The gas can be hot air, hydrogen, or helium. Hot-air balloons were among the earliest lighter-than-air aircraft. These balloons are open at one end. A burner close to the opening heats the air inside the balloon. Since hot air rises, the balloon rises up. A basket, called a gondola, holds the balloonist. Years ago, the gondola was made of lightweight wicker, but today synthetic materials are used. In time, people used buoyant gases other than hot air to fill these free-floating balloons.

A much more sophisticated lighter-than-air aircraft is the airship, also called a dirigible. Dirigible comes from a Latin word meaning "to direct." Dirigibles are powered by an engine and steered by a rudder. This is a big advantage over a balloon, which cannot be steered. Balloonists have to rely on air currents to take them where they want to go. The passengers and crew of a dirigible ride in an enclosed gondola suspended from an enormous, sealed balloon. The gas used in most modern dirigibles is helium.

Certainly the most famous airship in history was the ill-fated *Hindenburg*. Like the ocean liner Titanic, the *Hindenburg* was truly elegant. Passengers traveled in luxury, dining at linen-covered tables beside huge picture windows. What a view they must have had! Tragically, the *Hindenburg* had a fatal flaw. Instead of helium, the ship's balloon was filled with hydrogen, which is extremely flammable.

Nobody really knows what happened that Thursday in May 1937. Perhaps it was a spark that ignited the hydrogen, or maybe a structural failure. Whatever the cause, there was a huge explosion as the great airship neared the docking tower in Lakehurst, New Jersey, and the rear of the ship burst into flames. To those watching in horrified silence on the ground below, the *Hindenburg* seemed to vanish in an instant. Bits and pieces of the flaming wreckage floated to the ground like fiery snowflakes. One-third of those on board lost their lives. The glory years of the airships were over.

Go On

Now answer Numbers 21 through 28. Mark your answers on the Answer Sheet. Base your answers on the article "Lighter Than Air."

21 Read this sentence from the article.

Lighter-than-air aircraft drift in the air due to the buoyancy of a balloon.

The word *buoyancy* means the ability to

A. float.

B. steer.

C. speed up.

D. descend quickly.

22 A dirigible is different from a free-floating balloon in that

F. it contains a gondola.

G. it uses a gas that is lighter than air.

H. it relies on air currents to transport riders.

I. it is powered by an engine and steered by a rudder.

23 Why did the *Hindenburg* explode?

A. It crashed on the ground.

B. It collided with another aircraft.

C. Its gondola was not designed properly.

D. Its balloon was filled with flammable hydrogen.

24 What is this article mainly about?

F. hot-air ballooning

G. airships mistaken for UFOs

H. lighter-than-air aircraft

I. great airship disasters

Go On

Practice Test • 39

25 With which statement would the author of this article most likely agree?

A. Dirigibles are safer than hot-air balloons.

B. UFO buffs tend to speak before they are sure of their facts.

C. The ocean liner *Titanic* is more famous than the *Hindenburg*.

D. The *Hindenburg* would have exploded even if it had been filled with helium.

26 The author suggests that the glory years of airships ended because

F. dirigibles were uncomfortable to ride in.

G. people were afraid of dirigibles after the *Hindenburg* disaster.

H. pilots found it difficult to steer dirigibles.

I. they were replaced by airplanes.

27 Which of the following is an opinion from the article?

A. The first airship most people remember is the *Graf Zeppelin*, which flew on a regular basis between 1928 and 1937.

B. Years ago, the gondola was made of lightweight wicker, but today synthetic materials are used.

C. A much more sophisticated lighter-than-air aircraft is the airship, also called a dirigible.

D. Tragically, the *Hindenburg* had a fatal flaw.

28 Suppose there were no books in your library on the *Hindenburg* disaster. Which of these topics would be your best choice to look under in the card catalog or on the computer?

F. balloons, hot air

G. aircraft

H. disasters, marine

I. dirigibles

40 • Practice Test

Session 2

Read the story "The Marble Champ" before answering Numbers 29 through 36.

The Marble Champ

Gary Soto

Lupe Medrano, a shy girl who spoke in whispers, was the school's spelling bee champion, winner of the reading contest at the public library three summers in a row, blue ribbon awardee in the science fair, the top student at her piano recital, and the playground champion in chess. She was a straight-A student and—not counting kindergarten, when she had been stung by a wasp—never missed one day of elementary school. She had received a small trophy for this honor and had been congratulated by the mayor.

But though Lupe had a razor-sharp mind, she could not make her body, no matter how much she tried, run as fast as the other girls'. She begged her body to move faster, but could never beat anyone in the fifty-yard dash.

The truth was that Lupe was no good in sports. She could not catch a pop-up or figure out in which direction to kick the soccer ball. One time she kicked the ball at her own goal and scored a point for the other team. She was no good at baseball or basketball either, and even had a hard time making a hula hoop stay on her hips.

It wasn't until last year, when she was eleven years old, that she learned how to ride a bike. And even then she had to use training wheels. She could walk in the swimming pool but couldn't swim, and chanced roller skating only when her father held her hand.

"I'll never be good at sports," she fumed one rainy day as she lay on her bed gazing at the shelf her father had made to hold her awards. "I wish I could win at something, anything, even marbles."

At the word "marbles," she sat up. "That's it. Maybe I could be good at playing marbles." She hopped out of bed and rummaged through the closet until she found a can full of her brother's marbles. She poured the glass treasure on her bed and picked five of the most beautiful marbles.

She smoothed her bedspread and practiced shooting, softly at first so that her aim would be accurate. The marble rolled from her thumb and clicked against the targeted marble. But the target wouldn't budge. She tried again and again. Her aim became accurate, but the power from her thumb made the marble move only an inch or two. Then she realized that the bedspread was slowing the marbles. She also had to admit that her thumb was weaker than the neck of a newborn chick.

...Yes, she thought, I could play marbles, and marbles is a sport.

At that moment she realized that she had only two weeks to practice. The playground championship, the same one her brother had entered the previous year, was coming up. She had a lot to do.

...After practice, she squeezed an eraser for an hour. She ate dinner with her left hand to spare her shooting hand and said nothing to her parents about her dreams of athletic glory.

Practice, practice, practice. Squeeze, squeeze, squeeze. Lupe got better and beat her brother and Alfonso, a neighborhood kid who was supposed to be a champ.

...The day of the championship began with a cold blustery sky. The sun was a silvery light behind slate clouds.

...She beat her first opponent easily, and felt sorry for the girl because she didn't have anyone to cheer for her. Except for her sack of marbles, she was all alone. Lupe invited the girl, whose name was Rachel, to stay with them. She smiled and said, "OK." The four of them walked to a card table in the middle of the outfield where Lupe was assigned another opponent.

She also beat this girl, a fifth-grader named Yolanda, and asked her to join their group. They proceeded to more matches and more wins, and soon there was a crowd of people following Lupe to the finals to play a girl in a baseball cap. This girl seemed dead serious. She never even looked at Lupe.

"I don't know, Dad, she looks tough."

"You can do it," her father encouraged. "Just think of the marbles, not the girl, and let your thumb do the work."

The other girl broke first and earned one marble. She missed her next shot, and Lupe, one eye closed, her thumb quivering with energy, blasted two marbles out of the circle but missed her next shot. Her opponent earned two more before missing. She stamped her foot and said "Shoot!" The score was three to two in favor of Miss Baseball Cap.

The referee stopped the game. "Back up, please, give them room," he shouted. Onlookers had gathered too tightly around the players.

Lupe then earned three marbles and was set to get her fourth when a gust of wind blew dust in her eyes and she missed badly. Her opponent quickly scored two marbles, tying the game, and moved ahead six to five on a lucky shot. Then she missed, and Lupe, whose eyes felt scratchy when she blinked, relied on instinct and thumb muscle to score the tying point. It was now six to six, with only three marbles left. Lupe blew her nose and studied the angles. She dropped to one knee, steadied her hand, and shot so hard she cracked two marbles from the circle. She was the winner!

"The Marble Champ" by Gary Soto. Excerpt from BASEBALL IN APRIL AND OTHER STORIES, copyright © 1990 by Gary Soto, reprinted by permission of Harcourt, Inc.

Now answer Numbers 29 through 36. Mark your answers on the Answer Sheet. Base your answers on the story "The Marble Champ."

29 What is Lupe's biggest problem in the story?

A. She wants to be good at all sports.

B. She wants to win the marbles championship.

C. She wants to inpress the girl with the baseball cap.

D. She wants to beat someone in the fifty-yard dash.

30 Why does Lupe practice shooting marbles?

F. She hopes to beat the girl in the baseball cap.

G. She needs to improve her aim before the big match.

H. She wants to show her brother that girls can win at marbles.

I. She believes she can be the best marbles player in the world.

31 Read this sentence from the story.

She beat her first opponent easily, and felt sorry for the girl because she didn't have anyone to cheer for her.

Which of the following would be your *opponent*?

A. a girl playing on your soccer team

B. a boy running against you in a school election

C. a boy who asks for your help with his homework

D. a girl who comes in first in a race you are watching

32 Which word best describes Lupe's personality?

F. fearful

G. bold

H. calm

I. determined

Go On

44 • Practice Test

33 What is the best evidence that Lupe is a considerate person?

　A.　She plays marbles with her brother and Alfonso.

　B.　She waits to tell her parents about her dreams of winning.

　C.　She invites the girls whom she defeats to join her group.

　D.　She has a trophy for good attendance in elementary school.

34 What was the author's main purpose in writing this story?

　F.　to persuade readers to try to get involved with a sport of some kind

　G.　to describe to readers what goes on at a marbles championship

　H.　to explain to readers how to prepare for an athletic competition

　I.　to entertain readers with a story about a girl out to prove something

35 When Lupe's father tells her, "Just think of the marbles, not the girl," he means she should

　A.　be prepared to lose.

　B.　do anything to win.

　C.　concentrate on the game itself.

　D.　think about how pretty marbles are.

36 What is the message of this story?

　F.　Winning is the most important thing in life.

　G.　Being smart is more important than being good in sports.

　H.　If you work hard and concentrate on your goal, you will accomplish it.

　I.　A winner will have many friends, but a loser will have a hard time finding even one.

Read the article "Galileo and the Moons of Jupiter" before answering Numbers 37 through 42.

Galileo and the Moons of Jupiter

Tony Helies

Four hundred years ago, most people believed that Earth was the center of the universe. They thought that everything in the heavens, including the planets and the Sun, orbited our world.

An astronomer named Nicolaus Copernicus had written a book with a startling new theory: All planets, including Earth, orbit the Sun. Was Copernicus right or wrong?

In 1609, the Italian scientist and mathematician Galileo Galilei heard about a new device invented in Holland. Galileo thought it could help answer this question. The new instrument let the eye see distant objects as if they were nearby. It was the first telescope.

The early telescopes were made with two pieces of curved glass, called lenses, set into a metal tube. Telescope lenses are like the lenses in eyeglasses. Both types of lenses work on the same principle: Curved glass bends light. Telescope lenses are designed so this bending magnifies objects, making them look closer.

Galileo was excited by the idea of using this new invention to look at the heavens. But these early telescopes were not powerful enough for astronomy. So Galileo set about building a better one. He worked for six months, experimenting with different designs. His hard work paid off. The telescope he built made objects look thirty times closer than they did with the eye alone.

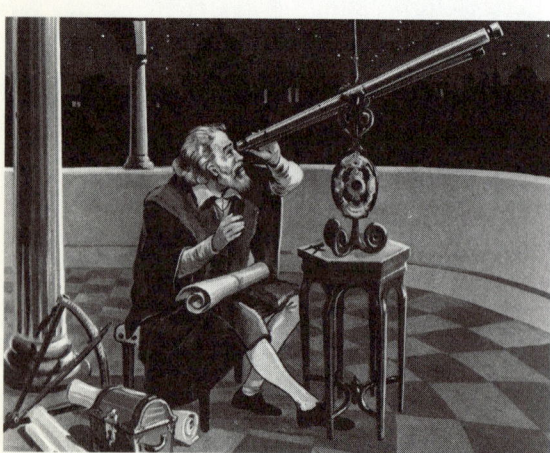

On January 7, 1610, Galileo pointed his telescope toward one of the brightest objects in the night sky, the planet Jupiter. On either side of Jupiter, he saw little points of light arranged in a straight line, two to the left and one to the right:

Galileo believed these were fixed stars, and expected they would remain in place as Jupiter moved across the sky.

The next night, he was surprised to find that the three stars were all to the right of Jupiter.

Galileo was puzzled. He had expected to find the stars farther to the left of Jupiter. What had caused them to move to the right? He waited impatiently to see where these stars would be on the third night, but cloudy skies blocked his view.

The next day, clear skies returned. Galileo was astonished by what he saw that night. Two of the stars had moved back to Jupiter's left and one had disappeared; Galileo suspected that the third object was behind Jupiter.

Over the next two nights, the three stars continued to move from one side of Jupiter to the other. Galileo now realized that the three points of light he was observing were orbiting Jupiter. They were moons, not stars.

Galileo had proved that not all heavenly bodies orbit Earth. The Earth was not at the center of everything after all. This was the first evidence supporting Copernicus's theory. It helped create our modern view of the universe.

On January 13, Galileo saw a fourth moon, which had been hidden behind Jupiter. These four moons—Io (EYE-oh), Europa (your-OH-pah), Ganymede (GAN-ih-meed), and Callisto (kuh-LIH-stoh)—are today known as the Galilean moons, in his honor.

Look at the sky on any clear, moonless night this month. The brightest object will be Jupiter. If you have a pair of binoculars, prop them against a wall or fence to steady them while you look at the planet. You may be able to see Jupiter's moons, just as Galileo did on a winter night more than 390 years ago.

"Galileo and the Moons of Jupiter" by Tony Helies. Copyright ©2002 by Highlights for Children, Inc., Columbus, Ohio.

Now answer Numbers 37 through 42. Mark your answers on the Answer Sheet. Base your answers on the article "Galileo and the Moons of Jupiter."

37 Read this sentence from the article.

The new instrument let the eye see distant objects as if they were nearby.

Which sentence below uses the word *instrument* with the same meaning as in the sentence from the article?

A. The violin is my favorite instrument in the orchestra.

B. A formal document such as a deed is called an instrument.

C. The test tube is an instrument used by research scientists.

D. The young king's wealthy uncle used his influence as an instrument to gain power.

38 Why did Galileo build his own telescope?

F. He could not buy a telescope from Holland.

G. He did not trust devices that he did not make himself.

H. He did not want anyone to study Jupiter before he did.

I. He could not get a telescope powerful enough for astronomy.

39 Which aspect of Galileo's discovery does the author emphasize in this article?

A. its role in forming the modern view of the universe

B. the importance of the discovery to Galileo's career

C. the difficulties Galileo had in making the telescope

D. its effect on other scientists of Galileo's day

40 What is the main idea of this article?

F. Galileo used the telescope he perfected to view the moons of Jupiter.

G. You can view Jupiter's moons just as Galileo did on a winter's night more than 390 years ago.

H. Galileo's discovery of how the moons of Jupiter orbit that planet gave support to Copernicus's theory.

I. There are four moons of Jupiter—Io, Europa, Ganymede, and Callisto.

41 Which of the following is the best evidence that Galileo was a free thinker?

A. He made his own telescope rather than using one invented in Holland.

B. He did not blindly accept the idea that the Earth was the center of the universe.

C. He believed Copernicus's theory about the universe right from the beginning.

D. He experimented with different designs before finally building his telescope.

42 What is the main organizational pattern used in this article?

F. cause-and-effect order

G. order of importance

H. chronological order

I. problem-solution order

Read the poem "Portrait by a Neighbour" before answering Numbers 43 through 48.

Portrait by a Neighbour

Edna St. Vincent Millay

Before she has her floor swept
Or her dishes done,
Any day you'll find her
A-sunning in the sun!

It's long after midnight
Her key's in the lock,
And you never see her chimney smoke
Till past ten o'clock!

She digs in her garden
With a shovel and a spoon,
She weeds her lazy lettuce
By the light of the moon.

She walks up the walk
Like a woman in a dream,
She forgets she borrowed butter
And pays you back in cream!

Her lawn looks like a meadow,
And if she mows the place
She leaves the clover standing
And the Queen Anne's lace!

"Portrait by a Neighbour" by Edna St. Vincent Millay. Copyright © 1922, 1950 by Edna St. Vincent Millay.

Now answer Numbers 43 through 48. Mark your answers on the Answer Sheet. Base your answers on the poem "Portrait by a Neighbour."

43 What does the first stanza tell you about the speaker's neighbor?

A. She feels restless.

B. She is a neat person.

C. She is a carefree person.

D. She does her chores right away.

44 What was the poet's reason for writing this poem?

F. to persuade readers to like her neighbor

G. to show how her neighbor does her gardening

H. to instruct readers on how to be a good neighbor

I. to entertain readers with things her neighbor does

45 If the poem needed a new title, which would be best?

A. "In the Garden"

B. "Lazy Days of Summer"

C. "A Lawn Like a Meadow"

D. "The Unusual Woman Next Door"

46 Read these lines from the poem.

**She walks up the walk
Like a woman in a dream,**

The speaker makes this comparison to show that her neighbor

F. sleepwalks during the day.

G. always walks slowly.

H. has many dreams.

I. often is lost in thought.

47 Which word best describes the tone of the poem?

A. formal

B. bittersweet

C. amused

D. ironic

48 The neighbor leaves the clover and Queen Anne's lace when she mows her lawn probably because she

F. thinks they are pretty.

G. wants to annoy the neighbors.

H. does not pay much attention as she mows.

I. does not know how to mow a lawn properly.

Read the passage from *The Story of My Life* **before answering Numbers 49 through 54.**

from The Story of My Life

Helen Keller

The morning after my teacher came, she led me into her room and gave me a doll. When I had played with it a little while, Miss Sullivan slowly spelled into my hand the word "d-o-l-l." I was at once interested in this finger play and tried to imitate it. When I finally succeeded in making the letters correctly, I was flushed with childish pleasure and pride. Running downstairs to my mother, I held up my hand and made the letters for "doll." I did not know that I was spelling a word or even that words existed; I was simply making my fingers go in monkey-like imitation. In the days that followed, I learned to spell in this uncomprehending way a great many words, among them "pin," "hat," "cup," and a few verbs like "sit," "stand," and "walk." But my teacher had been with me several weeks before I understood that everything has a name.

One day, while I was playing with my new doll, Miss Sullivan put a big rag doll into my lap, spelled "d-o-l-l," and tried to make me understand that "d-o-l-l" applied to both. Earlier that day we had a tussle over the words "m-u-g" and "w-a-t-e-r." Miss Sullivan had tried to impress it on me that "m-u-g" is mug and "w-a-t-e-r" is water, but I persisted in confounding the two. In despair, she had dropped the subject for the time, only to renew it at the first opportunity. I became impatient at her repeated attempts and, seizing the new doll, I dashed it upon the floor. I was keenly delighted when I felt the fragments of the broken doll at my feet. Neither sorrow nor regret followed my passionate outburst. I had not loved the doll. In the still, dark world in which I lived, there was no strong sentiment of tenderness. I felt my teacher sweep the fragments to one side of the hearth, and I had a sense of satisfaction that the cause of my discomfort was removed. She brought me my hat, and I knew I was going out into the warm sunshine. This thought, if a wordless sensation may be called a thought, made me hop and skip with pleasure.

We walked down the path to the well-house, attracted by the fragrance of the honeysuckle with which it was covered. Someone was drawing water, and my teacher placed my hand on the spout. As the cool stream gushed over one hand she spelled into the other the word "water," first slowly, then rapidly. Suddenly, I felt a misty consciousness as of something forgotten—a thrill of returning thought; and somehow, the mystery of language was revealed to me. I knew then that "w-a-t-e-r" meant the wonderfully cool something that was flowing over my hand. That living word awakened my soul, gave it light, hope, joy, set it free! There were barriers still, it is true, but barriers that could in time be swept away.

I left the well-house eager to learn. Everything had a name, and each name gave birth to a new thought. As we returned to the house, every object that I touched seemed to quiver with life. That was because I saw

everything with the strange new sight that had come to me. On entering the door I remembered the doll I had broken. I felt my way to the hearth and picked up the pieces. I tried vainly to put them together. Then my eyes filled with tears; for I realized what I had done, and for the first time I felt repentance and sorrow.

Now answer Numbers 49 through 54. Mark your answers on the Answer Sheet. Base your answers on the passage from *The Story of My Life.*

49 Why does Anne Sullivan give young Helen Keller a doll?

   A. to win the girl's affection

   B. to teach her to understand language

   C. to prevent a temper tantrum

   D. to play a game with the girl

50 What causes Helen Keller to smash the doll?

   F. She is tired of playing with the doll.

   G. She wants to get Sullivan's attention.

   H. She wants her mother to buy her another doll.

   I. She is annoyed that Sullivan tries to teach her new words.

51 What was the author's main purpose in writing this passage?

   A. to describe her teacher

   B. to entertain readers with an amusing story

   C. to explain how she learned that words stand for things

   D. to persuade readers that all handicaps can be overcome

52 What does Helen come to understand as a result of her experience at the well?

- F. Nature is beautiful.
- G. One must learn patience.
- H. Everyone makes mistakes.
- I. Language is a powerful tool.

53 How is Helen different at the end of the passage?

- A. She is able to see again.
- B. She is able to feel sorrow and guilt.
- C. She learns to appreciate nature.
- D. She has no further need for Anne Sullivan.

54 Read this sentence from the passage.

I learned to spell in this uncomprehending way a great many words, among them "pin," "hat," "cup," amd a few verbs like "sit," "stand," and "walk."

What is the meaning of the word *uncomprehending*?

- F. not caring
- G. not thinking
- H. not remembering
- I. not understanding

This is the end of the Practice Test.
Until time is called, go back and check your answers or answer questions you did not complete. When you have finished, close your Practice Test Book.

Name _____

Session 1

Answer all the questions that appear in the Reading Practice Test on this Answer Sheet.

1 Ⓐ Ⓑ Ⓒ Ⓓ	**2** Ⓕ Ⓖ Ⓗ Ⓘ	**3** Ⓐ Ⓑ Ⓒ Ⓓ
4 Ⓕ Ⓖ Ⓗ Ⓘ	**5** Ⓐ Ⓑ Ⓒ Ⓓ	**6** Ⓕ Ⓖ Ⓗ Ⓘ
7 Ⓐ Ⓑ Ⓒ Ⓓ	**8** Ⓕ Ⓖ Ⓗ Ⓘ	**9** Ⓐ Ⓑ Ⓒ Ⓓ
10 Ⓕ Ⓖ Ⓗ Ⓘ	**11** Ⓐ Ⓑ Ⓒ Ⓓ	**12** Ⓕ Ⓖ Ⓗ Ⓘ
13 Ⓐ Ⓑ Ⓒ Ⓓ	**14** Ⓕ Ⓖ Ⓗ Ⓘ	**15** Ⓐ Ⓑ Ⓒ Ⓓ
16 Ⓕ Ⓖ Ⓗ Ⓘ	**17** Ⓐ Ⓑ Ⓒ Ⓓ	**18** Ⓕ Ⓖ Ⓗ Ⓘ
19 Ⓐ Ⓑ Ⓒ Ⓓ	**20** Ⓕ Ⓖ Ⓗ Ⓘ	**21** Ⓐ Ⓑ Ⓒ Ⓓ
22 Ⓕ Ⓖ Ⓗ Ⓘ	**23** Ⓐ Ⓑ Ⓒ Ⓓ	**24** Ⓕ Ⓖ Ⓗ Ⓘ
25 Ⓐ Ⓑ Ⓒ Ⓓ	**26** Ⓕ Ⓖ Ⓗ Ⓘ	**27** Ⓐ Ⓑ Ⓒ Ⓓ
28 Ⓕ Ⓖ Ⓗ Ⓘ		

Answer Sheet

Grade 6

Session 2

Answer all the questions that appear in the Reading Practice Test on this Answer Sheet.

29. Ⓐ Ⓑ Ⓒ Ⓓ
30. Ⓕ Ⓖ Ⓗ Ⓘ
31. Ⓐ Ⓑ Ⓒ Ⓓ
32. Ⓕ Ⓖ Ⓗ Ⓘ
33. Ⓐ Ⓑ Ⓒ Ⓓ
34. Ⓕ Ⓖ Ⓗ Ⓘ
35. Ⓐ Ⓑ Ⓒ Ⓓ
36. Ⓕ Ⓖ Ⓗ Ⓘ
37. Ⓐ Ⓑ Ⓒ Ⓓ
38. Ⓕ Ⓖ Ⓗ Ⓘ
39. Ⓐ Ⓑ Ⓒ Ⓓ
40. Ⓕ Ⓖ Ⓗ Ⓘ
41. Ⓐ Ⓑ Ⓒ Ⓓ
42. Ⓕ Ⓖ Ⓗ Ⓘ
43. Ⓐ Ⓑ Ⓒ Ⓓ
44. Ⓕ Ⓖ Ⓗ Ⓘ
45. Ⓐ Ⓑ Ⓒ Ⓓ
46. Ⓕ Ⓖ Ⓗ Ⓘ
47. Ⓐ Ⓑ Ⓒ Ⓓ
48. Ⓕ Ⓖ Ⓗ Ⓘ
49. Ⓐ Ⓑ Ⓒ Ⓓ
50. Ⓕ Ⓖ Ⓗ Ⓘ
51. Ⓐ Ⓑ Ⓒ Ⓓ
52. Ⓕ Ⓖ Ⓗ Ⓘ
53. Ⓐ Ⓑ Ⓒ Ⓓ
54. Ⓕ Ⓖ Ⓗ Ⓘ